A Science Museum
illustrated booklet

SHIP MODELS

2: Sailing Ships from 1700 AD

by B. W. Bathe

Her Majesty's Stationery
Office London 1964

First published 1964
Third impression 1969

Introduction

The first part of this publication described and illustrated models of ships from the earliest times to 1700 AD and included a brief history of ship modelmaking for the same period. Part 2 deals with 18th and 19th century sailing warships and merchant ships; and in this introduction something of the later history of ship modelmaking is set forth.

The practice of making a scale model of a warship before the actual vessel was built continued into the 18th century. These official models were made to assist the Admiralty officials in their consideration of the type and size of ships that should be added to the Royal Navy.

An Admiralty order of 1716 required the construction of a model of every ship built or rebuilt and the Deptford Dockyard Letter Books preserved at the Public Record Office contain occasional references to models made under this order, for instance: 3rd July 1717—'In obedience to your Honrs. command we have more maturely reconsidered ye Solids or Models the Master Shipwright of Deptford hath prepared for the shape of H M Ship ye *Notingham* ordered to be rebuilt here and also ye solid of H M Ship *Revenge* rebuilding at Woolwich.' Another letter dated 21st November 1719 states: 'Pursuant to your Warrant of the 4th June 1716 I have prepared and sent herewith a Draught and a Solid shaped exactly according to it by which I design to rebuilt His Majesty's Ship *Chatham* but with due respect humbly submit the same to consideration for your directions thereon.'

That some of the models were rigged is evident from a letter dated the 17th November 1735: Honble. Sirs. There are wanting in His Majesty's Store here for completing a model or Solid of a First Rate Ship with Masts, Yards, Rigging and Blocks, Guns and Carriages and a proper Case for it, to be set in the Board Room of the Navy Office, in obedience to your Honours direction of the 11th October 1734 signify'd to the Master Shipwright for preparing the same. For the Model or Solid—Turkey Box, Peartree Leaves of $\frac{1}{8}$ in. thick, Do. dyed black, white ivory, Black Ebony, Cast brass for Guns according to the molds, Plate Brass, Belandine Silk, Best hard white Varnish, Camels hair brushes. For the case Mahogany Plank, 1 inch, Brass Locks Cupboard with Escutcheons 2, Hinges 5 pair, Spring Bolts, small, 4.

Unfortunately, little is known of the craftsmen who made these masterpieces, but the Deptford Letter books give details of a payment in 1741 of £77.18.4 to Mr Joseph Wade for the carved works of a model of a First Rate ship. These carvings are listed and included a bust of the King (George II), the Royal Arms and a 'Lyon for the Head with a crown and Locks of hair cutt through'. Another payment noted, also in 1741, is of £11.10.0 to a Mr Eplick for painting a model of a First Rate.

After about 1720 the method of making the official models was simplified. Instead of the framed construction (Plates 1, 2 and 3) the hull was fashioned from a solid block of wood, usually yellow pine, with much of the interior removed, leaving only a thin skin. Often the exterior form of this shell corresponded to the framing; and planking, of pear or boxwood, was applied as in actual wooden ship construction. In other cases the outward portions of the shell were lined and painted to represent planking. Many of the models were completed with the inboard details of each deck. Deck beams, carlings, knees, together with the cabin partitions, panelling, gratings, pumps and galley are shown (Plates 5, 6, 7, 8, 9, 10, 12 and 13).

The earlier practice of completely framed hulls was not, however, entirely abandoned; instances have been noticed of such models of mid-18th century ships and even much later contructions, but these were exceptions to the general practice and were probably intended to serve a special purpose.

Precise identification of Navy Board models presents an extremely difficult problem, but with a comprehensive knowledge of the changes in style of decoration and structural details it is possible by a close examination to determine the approximate period of many models.

The outbreak of war with France in 1793 brought an end to the practice of making elaborate models in the Royal dockyards, although simplified models such as half block models—particularly of captured enemy ships—were produced. However, during the long conflict with France a great number of ship models were made by prisoners-of-war confined in this country (Plate 14). The principal sources of these models were the prisons at Dartmoor, Porchester Castle and Norman Cross, near Peterborough, in which during the twenty-two years of war, prisoners were often confined for long periods. Official encouragement was given to the prisoners to exercise their industry and they were allowed to sell their handiwork. The ship models produced by the prisoners-of-war fall into two categories: those constructed in wood and those in bone, or sometimes in ivory. Those in wood show a marked superiority, both in proportions and attention to detail and can generally be accepted as reasonably faithful scale reproductions of particular classes of French ships. The bone models are usually of less reliable proportions and in extreme cases bear no relation to any actual ship. A peculiar feature is that each class of ship is usually represented by the largest type, for example the three-deckers are usually 120-gun ships, the two-deckers 80-gun ships, and frigates are commonly of the heaviest type carrying 50 guns.

With regard to materials, bone was easily obtained from the rations but other materials, such as hardwoods, ivory, whalebone and tortoiseshell must have been specially obtained from sources outside the prisons.

It is evident that there were among the prisoners a considerable number of adept craftsmen but under the circumstances of prison life and the limited facilities and equipment which were available, the delicate work found in the best of these models could have been achieved only by the exercise of great patience. The masts, spars and rigging of the models are so fragile that it would have been very difficult to preserve the larger models in the crowded conditions of prison life and most probably these models were made outside the prison by prisoners-of-war who were on parole.

After peace was restored in 1815 modelmaking was more generally resumed in the Royal Dockyards but most models were of the simpler form. Half block models fixed to a backboard became the common practice; these represented one half of the hull form only, and fittings and equipment were generally omitted. Considerable number of partial models, such as the head and stern only, were also produced for the purpose of illustrating the adoption of various structural improvements, such as the round bow introduced in line-of-battle ships in 1811, the circular stern introduced in 1817 by Sir Robert Seppings, Surveyor of the Navy, and the elliptical stern introduced ten years later.

Some more detailed models were made, typical examples being the models of the brig *Fantome*, 1839 (Plate 15) and the 90-gun ship *Albion*, 1842 (Plates 16 and 17).

Contemporary models of merchant vessels made before the middle of the 19th century are rare and the few models which exist do not usually compare in quality with the models of warships made in the naval dockyards. The Honourable East India Company held almost a complete monopoly during its many years of trading activity and it is surprising that so few detailed builders' models seem to have been produced for the Company which chartered so many vessels. Most of the contemporary models of East Indiamen which do exist seem to be the work of capable but not expert craftsmen.

The era of the famous tea clippers was characterized by competition among builders to produce superior designs and an increase in shipbuilding activity. This explains the existence of a large number of models of that period. Usually these followed the pattern of the earlier Admiralty practice of half-block models, but complete hull models gradually became more numerous and occasionally a completely rigged example survives.

Some really fine scale reproductions of vessels were built in the yards of important shipbuilding firms right up to the end of the 19th century, after which sail gave way to steam for large ship propulsion.

More recently a number of very fine scale models have been produced by professional and amateur model makers. The models of the whaler *Alice Mandell* (Plate 18) and the *Cutty Sark* (Plate 19) are examples of the skill of 20th century model makers.

In contrast to the lack of evidence on ships of the middle ages, which only permits the construction of the conjectural models described in Part 1 of this publication, and to the very limited knowledge of early 18th century merchant ships; information on warships of the 18th and 19th century is extensive, and is supplemented by the many accurate contemporary models which still exist. In addition a very large collection of contemporary Admiralty draughts of all classes of warships is preserved at the National Maritime Museum, Greenwich.

1 90-Gun Ship c.1706

This very fine model represents a Second Rate of 90 guns built in accordance with the Established dimensions laid down in 1706.

From 1677, for a period of about 70 years, each new assessment of naval needs became known as the 'Establishment' of that period. The shipbuilding Establishments authorized standard dimensions for every class of warship for the Royal Navy. The dates of these Establishments were 1677, 1691, 1706, 1719, 1745 and further revisions were proposed in 1733 and 1741. In spite of a gradual increase in the sizes of the vessels of each class, the rigid specification of the Establishments retarded the progress of English naval architecture; and after 1745 the designers and shipbuilders were allowed a much freer hand in interpreting the requirements of the fighting service.

The Established dimensions of a 90-gun ship at this date were: burden 1551 tons; length of gun-deck 162 ft; length of keel for tonnage 132 ft; breadth 47 ft; depth in hold 18.5 ft.

The model formerly belonged to Daniel Finch (1647-1730) 2nd Earl of Nottingham and 6th Earl of Winchelsea, who held a number of high offices of state between 1681 and 1716. It was received at the Museum in a very damaged condition, but was completely restored in the seven year period from 1931 to 1938.

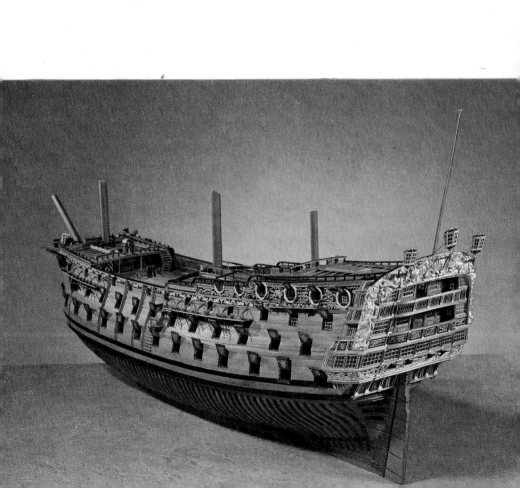

2 90-Gun Ship, bows

A noticeable constructional feature of three-deckers during the reigns of Anne and George I was the unusually deep heads. These presented an appearance of clumsiness, largely owing to the lowness of the cheeks, and as a result, the four-railed head illustrated in the model was introduced.

Although an Admiralty order of 1703 severely restricted the profuse carved and gilded work, then so prominent, it only remained effective for a very brief period. And so, several years prior to the death of Anne in 1714, carving and gilding again came into vogue but was not as elaborate as that of the earlier Stuart period.

The painted decorations of the model show a style of naval ornament which was peculiar to the early years of the 18th century. Chinese figures were painted on the counters, the beakhead bulkheads and the undersides of the gun-port lids. This Chinese influence is also shown in the design of the carved lion figurehead, where it persisted for some time after it had disappeared from the painted work.

3　20-Gun Ship c.1719

This contemporary model shows one of the smaller types of vessels built for the Royal Navy. It represents a Sixth Rate of 20 guns built to the dimensions of the 1719 Establishment; the rigging except for minor renewals is original.

The design of these Sixth Rates seems to have been derived from that of the earlier Fifth Rates of 32 guns, to which they closely approximated in dimensions; but all lower deck gunports disappeared and only one midship port aside was retained, to serve as a ballast port.

The sweep-ports, 18 aside on the lower deck, recall the fact that oars were then commonly used in a great number of the lighter vessels and did not finally disappear from the smaller frigates until the early years of the 19th century.

As some 21 vessels of this class were built between 1719 and 1727 exact identification is difficult, but it is possible that the model represents the first of the class H M S *Blandford* built in 1719. The dimensions of the *Blandford* were: burden 375 tons; length of gundeck 106 ft; length of keel for tonnage 87.3 ft; breadth 28.5 ft; depth in hold 9.2 ft.

4 Bucentaur 1728

From very early times elaborately decorated vessels have been used for religious and state occasions.

This contemporary model, made in Venice and dated 1727, represents the last of the *Bucentaurs*, State Barges of the Doges of Venice. Since 1177 a succession of these vessels had been employed for the ceremonial marriage between the Republic and the Adriatic, which was celebrated annually on the Feast of the Ascension.

The *Bucentaur* represented by the model was laid down in 1722 in the Arsenal of Venice, and was launched in 1728. As was usual with state barges, the vessel, which was about 114 ft long, was built in archaic style and preserved much of the earlier tradition of her predecessors. She was propelled by 21 oars aside with four men to each oar and except for her shallow draught and gorgeous awning and other decorations she greatly resembled the Mediterranean galleasses of the 17th and 18th centuries.

The *Bucentaur* was stripped of her gold ornaments and partially destroyed during the French occupation of Venice in 1798 and was broken up in 1824.

5   50-Gun Ship c.1736

At this period 50-gun ships, with two decks and a poop, were considered particularly suitable for prolonged cruises.

This contemporary model probably represents the *Gloucester*, one of a squadron which, under Commodore Anson in the *Centurion*, sailed in September 1740 for an expedition to the Pacific which culminated in a voyage round the world. After accompanying Anson during a great part of the voyage the *Gloucester* was severely damaged in a storm in July 1742 and was later destroyed by Anson's orders.

The *Gloucester* was the first of a class of nine 50-gun ships built between 1736 and 1742, according to the dimesions authorised in the Establishment proposed in 1733.

With a breadth of 38.5 ft and a gun-deck 134 ft long this class of 50-gun ships was of 853 tons burden and carried an armament of twenty-two 18-pdr guns on the lower gun-deck, twenty-two 9-pdrs on the upper gun-deck, with four 6-pdrs on the quarter deck, and two on the forecastle.

6 50-Gun Ship, bows

The splendid gilded lion which forms the figure-head of this 50-gun ship still retains something of the Chinese appearance which was introduced into the ornamentation of ships of the Royal Navy about 1700. This Chinoiserie has, however, completely disappeared from the beakhead bulkhead and broadside which are decorated with a frieze of painted foliage and trophies of arms.

As can be seen in the plate opposite, the bowsprit was secured by the knightheads, massive timbers placed just forward of the beakhead bulkhead; and by the bowsprit gammoning, a lashing of strong rope between the bowsprit and the stem-head.

7 50-Gun Ship, main and mizen masts

The masts, yards and rigging of this model are also contemporary
and give a very accurate representation of the usage of the period.
At this date the mizen mast of a 50-gun ship was not lengthened
by a top-gallant mast and consequently, in addition to the fore and
aft lateen sail set on the long and cumbersome lateen yard, it only
carried a square topsail.

Several features of the rigging are clearly shown in the plate
opposite, for instance the shrouds—ropes from the mast set up
with deadeyes and lanyards to the side of vessel—which sup-
ported the masts; and the crows-foot—the system of small ropes
running from the fore edge of the top to a block on the mast stay—
which prevented the foot of the topsail getting under the top.

8 H M S 'Achilles' 1757

This contemporary model is typical of the 60-gun ships built between 1750 and 1760 and represents the *Achilles* built by Messrs J. Barnard and Turner, at Harwich, and launched in 1757.

The model shows that by the middle of the 18th century, the poop and forecastle had become proportionally longer in ships of this class than in the earlier 60-gun ships; and that narrow permanent gangways connected the quarter-deck and forecastle, but athwart ships beams were not yet fitted in the waist.

The fore and main channels—the platforms which served to extend the shrouds of those masts—occupy a position level with the quarter-deck and forecastle, an improvement which had been introduced into two-deckers about 1745. This change was of great value in decreasing the impact of heavy seas on the channels when the weather was bad, and so reducing damage to the shrouds which stayed the mast.

9 H M S 'Achilles', bows

During the reign of Charles II, men-of-war other than First Rates used the crowned lion as a figure-head and it would seem that it was not until the last decade of the 17th century that the privilege of individual figure-heads was extended to Second Rates. In 1727 the Admiralty authorized the use of appropriate figures in the smaller ships and by about 1760 individual figures were fitted to most ships.

The identification of this model of a 60-gun ship is confirmed by the full length carved figure of the Greek hero Achilles at the bow. Additional carving appears on the port and starboard trail boards, which can be seen below the feet of the figure; and at the end of the catheads, the projecting timbers used as a form of davit for the anchor.

The stern of this model of a two-decker has a single, open balustrad-ed stern-walk with 'open quarters' that is open access to the port and starboard quarter-galleries.

Stern-walks were introduced again about 1680 for the larger vessels. From this date right up to the end of the 18th century it was the usual practice to have two stern-walks on a three-decker and one on a two-decker; but divergences do occur, as there are in-stances of 70-gun ships with two-stern walks. The 50-gun ships normally had one until 1733, but on the other hand some 60-gun ships had no stern-walks. They were never fitted to any smaller English men-of-war.

11 Mediterranean Chebec c.1760

Throughout the 18th century, as in earlier centuries, Barbary corsairs operating from the North African ports were an almost constant threat to merchant ships in the Mediterranean.

One of the vessels much favoured by these corsairs was the Chebec. Although of galley form and provided with nine oar-ports aside, the chebec was designed for sailing rather than rowing.

The three large fore-and-aft lateen sails gave the vessel fast sailing qualities, which, together with the relatively heavy armament of four 12-pdr, sixteen 6-pdr and eight 3-pdr guns, produced a most efficient and formidable craft.

That the design of the chebec was, in suitable conditions, particularly successful for patrol and similar duties is shown by the fact that they were employed by the Spanish and French forces in the Mediterranean and a very similar type of vessel was built for the Russian and Swedish navies for use in the Baltic.

The name frigate was given to various types of warships at different periods. However, the best known application was to the 18th century vessel specially designed for scouting, convoy duties and attacks on enemy merchant ships, which carried its main armament on a single gun-deck.

During the first half of the 18th century the largest vessels in the Royal Navy to carry their main armament in this manner were the Sixth Rates of 24 guns.

In 1757 a new class of vessel was introduced, the 32-gun frigate and by the end of the century the fleet contained frigates of 40, 38, 36, 32, 28, 24, and 20 guns.

Between 1777 and 1785 some thirty 28-gun frigates were built and the model most probably represents one of the latest of the class, the *Ariel* built at Dover in 1785.

The plate opposite shows the main and mizen masts and the quarter-deck of the model. It will be seen that on these frigates the gangways between quarter-deck and forecastle were still rather narrow and the beams in the waist, on which the boats and spare spars were stowed, were removable. On the mizen mast, the long gaff and even longer boom were used to spread the large driver, a sail which had taken the place of the earlier lateen mizen sail.

13 Naval Cutter c.1790

Cutters, fast sailing vessels much used for patrol and dispatch services in the late 18th and early 19th centuries, were introduced into the Royal Navy about 1750.

The early cutter-rig, which probably developed from that of the late 17th century Dutch yacht, consisted of a very large mainsail with gaff and boom; a square topsail; a foresail on the forestay; and a large jib on the long bowsprit. It differed from the sloop-rig then in use in that the forestay led to the stem, and the bowsprit was a horizontal 'running' spar which could be housed; while the forestay of a sloop-rigged vessel led to the bowsprit, which was a standing spar and was also steeved. Further, the 18th century sloop-rigged vessels were usually fitted with a beak and figure-head, while the naval cutters had always a plain straight stem.

The model represents one of the larger naval cutters of about 151 tons burden, with gun-deck length of 69 ft and an armament of twelve guns, two carronades and two swivels. The hull is of typical cutter form, clincher-built, with steep floors and its greatest breadth at the stepping of the mast.

14 French 120-Gun Ship c.1800

This model is a fine example of the ship models made in bone by French prisoners-of-war in this country during the period 1793-1815.

The model is unusually large for prisoner-of-war work and is of particularly good craftsmanship. The carvings, deck fittings and rigging, all typically French in style, are very detailed; and some of the guns are mounted with concealed springs so that they may be run in and out of the gun-ports by pulling a cord.

As prisoners-of-war did not have scale draughts from which to work, their models can only be regarded as representative; and the names inscribed on them must not be taken too seriously, for they were often chosen to facilitate the sale of the models.

In this case the model is inscribed on the stern with the name *Ocean*; but it does not accurately represent the French 120-gun ship of that name launched at Brest in 1790.

15 H M Brig 'Fantome' 1839

Between 1800 and 1830 a number of improvements in the design and construction of warships took place, which produced men-of-war of very much stronger construction than had previously been possible. Sir William Symonds, who was appointed Surveyor of the Navy in 1832, while retaining this solid construction endeavoured to produce vessels capable of greater sailing speed. In order to do this he designed vessels with a greater beam and an under-water body with a very pronounced 'V' cross section. Ships built to this design were undoubtedly fast sailers but had a tendency to heel excessively in a strong wind.

The *Fantome*, launched at Chatham in 1838, was one of a class of fourteen 16-gun brigs built to this new design. The armament of the *Fantome* consisted of four 32-pdr guns and twelve 32-pdr carronades.

Naval brigs of this period were fully square-rigged on both masts and the foot of the large gaff-sail was extended by a boom.

Brigs were used as training ships in the Royal Navy for many years after steam vessels came into general use.

The 90-gun ships of the *Albion* class were the largest two-decker men-of-war built in this country during the sailing ship period. The vessels were of 3111 tons burden, with a breadth of 60 ft and a gun-deck 204 ft long.

In size and standard of masting these huge two-deckers were on a par with the largest three-deckers, but they came so late in the era of sail that only two were completed as sailing ships.

The round bow—built right up to the forecastle level—shown on the model, was first introduced for the smaller vessels of the Royal Navy as early as 1732. It was first fitted to a two-decker in 1801 and in 1811 was authorized for all classes of naval ships. The use of the round bow, besides making the vessel much drier in a head sea, increased the number of guns which a large ship could bring to bear on either bow.

H M S *Albion* was designed by Sir William Symonds, Surveyor of the Navy from 1832 to 1847, and launched at Devenport in 1842. In 1861 she was converted into a steamship with screw propulsion.

17 H M S 'Albion', stern

Marked changes in the designs of the sterns of warships took place in the early years of the 19th century.

The older form of square stern made men-of-war very vulnerable to attack from astern. This weakness was remedied to some extent, by the introduction in 1819 of the circular stern, designed by Sir Robert Seppings, Surveyor of the Navy. This change in form, in which the sudden change of curvature on the quarter was done away with, had the advantage of giving greater strength and resistance to the raking fire of an enemy ship astern and enabled guns to be mounted on each quarter. The elliptical stern, shown on this model of the *Albion*, was first introduced in 1827 and was regarded as a further improvement.

The elliptical stern made possible the return to quarter-galleries of almost the old-fashioned form. In two-deckers one, and in three-deckers two, projecting galleries were added which bore some resemblance to the open stern-galleries of the 18th century; but the severity of the decoration is very different to the ornate style of the earlier period.

18 Whaling Ship 'Alice Mandell' 1851

The American whaling industry was particularly flourishing in the middle of the 19th century. In 1857 over 300 whalers were operating from New Bedford alone.

The whaling ships of this period were usually designed with somewhat less beam and with finer under-water lines than vessels intended for the merchant service generally. These features gave the whalers sailing qualities which their heavy appearance tended to belie. The model represents the New Bedford whaling ship *Alice Mandell* built in 1851. The vessel made two whaling voyages only, on the second of which she was wrecked in the China Seas in March 1857.

The *Alice Mandell* was built of wood, copper sheathed below the waterline and ship-rigged, She was equipped with seven whale-boats, five carried on heavy wooden davits and two spare boats on skids aft of the mainmast. It was in these whale-boats that the actual pursuing and harpooning of the whale was accomplished. A portion of the starboard bulwark amidships was removable to facilitate cutting up the whale, the large tackle over the main hatch being used to hoist the strip of blubber as it was removed from the carcass lying in the water alongside the ship. A 'cutting-stage', rigged outboard. assisted in this process. The oil was extracted from the blubber in a brick oven fitted with iron vats, known as the 'try-works', situated on deck abaft the foremast.

19 Clipper Ship 'Cutty Sark' 1869

After the slow evolution of some 5000 years, the sailing ship reached near perfection in the clipper ship of the mid-19th century. In the 1840's American shipbuilders began designing large sailing ships on the lines of the Baltimore brigs and schooners, long famous for their speed. These American vessels established a great reputation for speed and their finer lines had considerable influence on the design of the British-built ships which succeeded them.

The only surviving example of the clippers is the *Cutty Sark*, now preserved in a dry-dock at Greenwich. This vessel, designed by Hercules Linton, was built by Messrs Scott and Linton at Dumbarton in 1869 for the China trade. Although she was famous as one of the fastest of the Tea Clippers, it was later, when engaged in the Australian wool trade, that she attained her greatest reputation.

The *Cutty Sark* was of composite construction. This method of construction consisted in making all the interior framework of the ship, frames, deck beams, pillars, etc. of iron but then planking the hull with wood which below the waterline, was sheathed with copper.

With a length of 212.5 ft and a breadth of 36 ft, the *Cutty Sark* was ship-rigged, that is with square sails on all three masts. The lower masts were of rolled iron and she was fitted with double topsails on each mast.

20   Schooner 'E. W. Morrison' c.1870

The schooner rig, which is probably of Dutch origin, is essentially American in development, although instances have been found of small English two-masted fore-and-aft rigged vessels as early as the beginning of the 18th century. By the middle of the century, the schooner had become the prevalent type of small coaster through-out the east coast of North America, from Newfoundland to the West Indies; and when, at a later date, the rig became common in the British Isles, it was from the American schooners that the designs were copied.

The fore-and-aft rig proved itself particularly suited to coasting work under variable winds; although unsatisfactory for long ocean voyages, which generally coincided with favourable winds. The earlier schooners retained some of the square sails of the three-masted ship, but by the middle of the 19th century the Americans had entirely discarded square topsails.

By the beginning of the 20th century very large American schooners were in use, carrying four, five, six and in one instance seven masts. Two, three and four-masted schooners were employed in the grain, coal and ore trades on the Great Lakes of North America. The model is of the *E. W. Morrison*, a three-masted schooner built of wood about 1870 and belonging to the Port of Chicago.

Science Museum illustrated booklets

Other titles in this series:

Timekeepers Clocks, watches, sundials, sand-glasses[†]
Ship Models Part 1 : From earliest times to 1700 AD[†]
Ship Models Part 3 : British Small Craft[*]
Ship Models Part 4 : Foreign Small Craft[*]
Railways Part 1 : To the end of the 19th century[*]
Chemistry Part 1 : Chemical Laboratories and Apparatus to 1850[*]
Chemistry Part 2 : Chemical Laboratories and Apparatus from 1850[*]
Chemistry Part 3 : Atoms, Elements and Molecules[†]
Chemistry Part 4 : Making Chemicals[†]
Aeronautics Part 1 : Early Flying up to the Reims meeting[*]
Aeronautics Part 2 : Flying since 1913[*]
Power to Fly Aircraft Propulsion[*]
Aeronautics Objets d'Art, Prints, Air Mail[*]
Lighting Part 1 : Early oil lamps, candles[*]
Lighting Part 2 : Gas, mineral oil, electricity[†]
Making Fire Wood friction, tinder boxes, matches[*]
Cameras Photographs and Accessories[*]
Agriculture Hand tools to Mechanization[*]
Fire Engines and other fire-fighting appliances[*]
Astronomy Globes, Orreries and other Models[†]
Surveying Instruments and Methods[†]
Physics for Princes The George III Collection[†]

Published by
Her Majesty's Stationery Office
and obtainable from the
Government Bookshops listed
on cover page iv (post orders
to PO Box 569, London SE1)

*5s each (by post 5s 5d)
†6s each (by post 6s 5d)

Printed in England for
Her Majesty's Stationery Office
by W. Heffer & Sons Ltd
Cambridge

Dd. 138218 K120